75929

F
128.63 Rosebrock, Ellen
R67   South street
1977

FEB 23 '79	DATE DUE		

SOUTH STREET

A PHOTOGRAPHIC GUIDE TO
NEW YORK CITY'S HISTORIC SEAPORT

SOUTH STREET

A PHOTOGRAPHIC GUIDE TO
NEW YORK CITY'S HISTORIC SEAPORT

Text by Ellen Fletcher Rosebrock
Photographs by Edmund V. Gillon, Jr.

DOVER PUBLICATIONS, INC.
NEW YORK

Published in Canada by General Publishing Company, Ltd., 30 Lesmill Road, Don Mills, Toronto, Ontario.
Published in the United Kingdom by Constable and Company, Ltd., 10 Orange Street, London WC2H 7EG.

South Street: A Photographic Guide to New York City's Historic Seaport is a new work, first published by Dover Publications, Inc., in 1977. Some of the material contained in this edition originally appeared in *Walking Around in South Street: Discoveries in New York's Old Shipping District,* published in 1974 by the South Street Seaport Museum, 16 Fulton Street, New York City 10038.

International Standard Book Number: 0-486-23396-0
Library of Congress Catalog Card Number: 76-62807

Manufactured in the United States of America
Dover Publications, Inc.
180 Varick Street, New York, N.Y. 10014

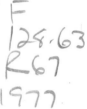

Acknowledgments

This guide to the neighborhood of the South Street Seaport Museum could not have been written without the work of many people. First there was research done by Lee Roberts and Nancy Steinke for the New York City Landmarks Preservation Commission. On their report most subsequent work was based. There was still more research in which Dan Brunetto, Alan Burnham, Margot Gayle, Regina Kellerman, Ellen Kramer, Lee Roberts and Val Wenzel participated more than generously. Bronson Binger and Peter Stanford proposed that a guide be written, and gave the kind of encouragement that was absolutely necessary to put the facts down on paper. Norma Stanford and David Canright did artwork for the South Street Seaport Museum's original edition (1974). Terry Walton edited the manuscript and advised on its original production. And without the aid of the New York State Council on the Arts, who encouraged the writing of this guide from the beginning, none of the final fact-gathering and writing would have been possible. For this new edition, Hayward Cirker drew the author's attention past the old peaked roofs and the chimneys of the 19th-century buildings to the crested towers and boxy turrets of the downtown skyscrapers that form such an elegant backdrop to the South Street neighborhood. And Edmund V. Gillon, Jr., in his wonderful photographs, caught the substance of the old district's visible history.

Preface

Echoing to sailors' songs and draymen's curses, old brick streaked by many rains and windows dazzled by rising suns across the tides of the East River, the old buildings of the South Street waterfront have survived to our day. They house lively memories and meanings. They survive from a time when words and deeds were bolder in New York—when people talked with a salt savor to their words, a wholeness and bite in discourse as one can catch in old papers of the time; and they walked with a proprietary swagger, a sense of owning and belonging that you catch, in old photographs, in the stance of the hostler and the merchant prince alike. Mutual respect in a class-conscious society? Or merely a kind of settled dependence, which one can see symbolized in the old buildings of South Street, leaning against each other for mutual support?

Who knows? The fact is that the historic neighborhood survives to be enjoyed today. The story of people's work before our time also survives, and is celebrated here. We know General Ebenezer Stevens who won glory in the War for Independence by his countinghouses on Front and South Streets where he based his traffic in exotic liquors from 1798. There are others, too, whose lives touched here once, adding little by little to that composite character that the newest visitor can feel walking into our South Street neighborhood, once famous around the world as the "street of ships."

South Street is a monumental collection of ships and buildings weathering some kind of passage through the seas of time. It is a most visible argument in favor of things being (in an overcalculating society) a little more natural, a little more mutually dependent, a little out of plumb.

Hurrah for old humanity! Let us honor its cause here in South Street, where its labors are so clearly, vividly, memorably expressed in the shapes of the housing and sea chariots of an earlier day. Let us find new meanings in these old roots, so we can get on with the work of the city today with a little more grace, a little more dignity, a new sense of joy in the work. The South Street Seaport Museum plans to reclaim for the purpose some of these ancient, leaning structures—to stabilize them, not to rebuild them, but definitely to care for them.

And if you care to be part of these efforts, join the Museum! You'll find in the words of the old story, "a hearty welcome waiting." Your help is needed, because our buildings, our ships, our story have no meaning and no future without you.

PETER STANFORD

v

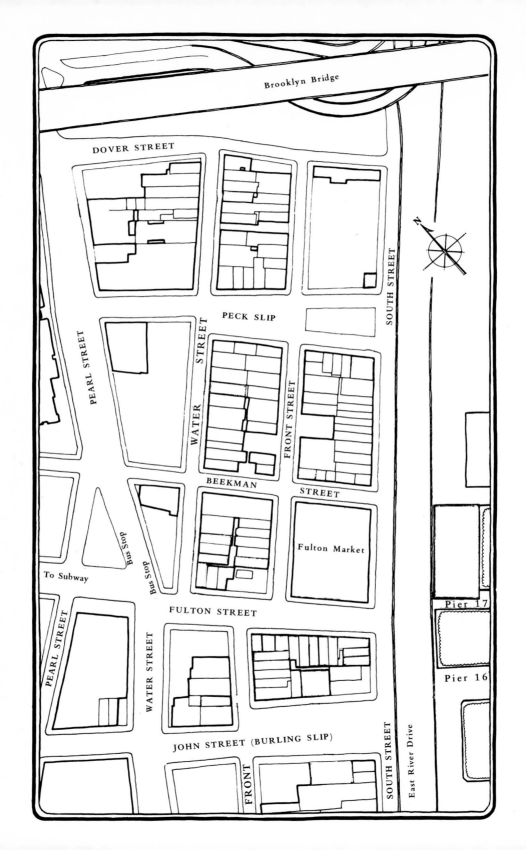

Introduction

"One needs to come down to the river quays to see the greatness of New York," a visitor said of South Street in 1856. And you can come down to the river quays today, at the South Street Seaport Museum, to sense what it was like in this seaport city when sailing ships belted the tip of Manhattan with a forest of masts. Those ships arrived from port cities on every ocean, bringing mountains of goods packed solidly in barrels and bales to merchants who worked in the very buildings that stand today along the streets of the neighborhood, shown in the photographs of this book.

As you look at these photographs—or walk through the stone-paved streets themselves—your first impression may be one of ranges of tired old buildings, mossy, grayed, and often out of plumb. But here and there a beautiful detail—a glimpse of rosy, handmade brick, perhaps; a delicate, arched doorway with brownstone trim; the brittle shimmer of old glass newly washed—suggests a visual and historical richness that invites closer inspection.

The seven-block survival of warehouses and stores in the museum's neighborhood has not always been so distinct from the rest of the city, but once directly reflected the rise and progress of the downtown business community, sharing its booms and depressions and echoing them in the fortunes of its occupants and its buildings.

The South Street–Front Street–Water Street strip on the East River is all "made" land, created from tidelands by successive periods of landfill and wharf building between 1686 and 1820. The strip was, during its 19th-century history, literally the gateway to the city, wrapping the grander inner portions: Wall Street with its handsome Georgian and Greek Revival buildings, the financial palaces of an earlier day; Broadway with its brilliant retail shops (extravagantly lit with gas from an early date, and kept open late into the night); and, closer to the East River shipping center, the wholesale shops of Pearl Street, "the richest street in the city."

Little remains of the commercial center of 19th-century New York—an occasional high-style landmark well cared for, and scattered single and grouped buildings which to varying degrees retain evidence of an early origin. Continued prosperity and the New York characteristic of pursuing progress have replaced most of the buildings in downtown New York several times over.

If you approach the South Street Seaport Museum afoot from the inner downtown streets, your emergence into breeze and light and salty air might give you your first perception of what it was like in the waterfront district of the 19th century. Here the sun shines at midday into the narrowest streets, the sky somehow seems closer overhead than in the downtown canyons. Here at South Street we can see how the city was supposed to look when street widths were determined in the 18th and early 19th centuries.

To prepare for your walk, think of the early, hurried days when these streets were laid out, when the land-hungry city men pushed their shores street by street out into land claimed from the harbor. If some of these buildings seem a bit cracked and leaning, it's because the merchants who built them were in such a hurry to get going that they couldn't wait for their artificial land to finish settling before they framed up their stores and countinghouses and

FULTON FERRY TERMINAL *(D. T. VALEN-TINE'S MANUAL,* 1864). In 1814 the Fulton Ferry, running across the East River to Brooklyn, established the end of Fulton Street (then Beekman's Slip) as its Manhattan terminal. The first ferry house, a classical wooden structure, was replaced by this cast-iron building in 1863.

sank their stone foundations into the shifting mud of the landfill.

To get to the beginning of all this, think back for a moment further than these streets themselves, to the first European involvement with Manhattan Island. Early in the 17th century, even before there were houses here, or a fort, there was the harbor itself and there was trade. At the time of the burning of the *Tiger* in 1614 we know that at least a dozen Dutch ships were using the harbor on trading missions with the Indians. Only the rudest of shelters welcomed the Dutchmen on Manhattan's shores, but their commercial visits here were many.

During the 17th century the little outpost grew from a lonely colony in the woods to a respectable commercial town. The English took possession of New York in 1664, and thereafter it grew steadily on its trade, stimulated by the wars with the French over Canada. Early growth was quiet, and its process was interrupted by the American Revolution.

It was after 1783 (the evacuation of the British troops from New York) that the city began to express itself in a startling way. Not a month after the evacuation merchants were sending out ships on ambitious globe-spanning junkets. Through the last decades of the 18th century, New York prospered, and by 1800 had become America's major seaport town.

New York had just begun to climb in 1800. From then until the beginning of the Civil War, the city, firmly rooted in its mercantile tradition, was what its harbor had made it—and its harbor was at South Street. There the merchants had their tall, proud countinghouses from whose small-paned windows they surveyed the channel waters and the ships moored along the wharves. Running back from South Street the slips and lanes lined with smaller houses led to Front and Water Streets, where the tradesmen and the warehouses (to say nothing of the saloons and boardinghouses) completed the waterfront community.

Following the War of 1812 South Street and New York grew apace. In January of 1818 the Black Ball Line of Liverpool packets (the first regular transatlantic freight and passenger line) began sailing from South Street just south of Peck Slip, near the present Pier 17. "From the sailing of this packet," wrote seedsman Grant Thorburn in his memoirs, "we may date the day whence the commerce of New York began to increase seven-fold." In 1825 the opening of the Erie Canal channeled farm and industrial produce from the Middle West through New York harbor and out in the city's ships for export. Five hundred new mercantile firms were founded in New York during that year alone, but as Robert G. Albion reminds us in his classic *Rise of New York Port,* it was South Street—the seaport—that created the canal, that generated the money and the business to build it: it was not the canal that created South Street.

During the second half of the 1820s nearly all accounts of the city described the nearly unnavigable state of the sidewalks due to mud and the impediments of successful commerce. Crates, barrels, boxes and carts burst from every overloaded store to pile on the street. The 1840s and 1850s saw the high noon of New York's maritime empire. The China trade, led by A. A. Low & Brothers, infused the streets with exotic glamor. Japan was opened in 1854, and clippers from this port were carrying thousands of settlers to California. The South Street countinghouses, formerly occupied by one or two firms, began to crowd up; sail makers, riggers, figurehead carvers and other waterfront businesses joined the merchants in their buildings.

From the 1860s on, the neighborhood declined in importance. The new giant steamships went to deepwater piers on the North River (Hudson). The commercial center—except for the insurance industry around John Street, the investment community centering on Wall Street, the great shipping firms near the island tip, clustering round Whitehall Street and lower Broadway—crept toward midtown. A kind of raffishness replaced early commercial opulence, and as the sailing ships departed, one by one, on their last voyages, leaving behind in the towers of Lower Manhattan a world-renowned monument to the business they'd brought here, a kind of parochial somnolence began to replace the bustle and worldwide outlook of an earlier age.

Today the old seaport neighborhood stirs to new, intensely local but also cosmopolitan vitality as the South Street Seaport Museum brings together visitors, ships, discourse, educational programs and the reviving bustle of shops and eateries which will make the area again a market of goods, of ideas—and of people.

Begin the walk on Fulton Street near the corner of Front.

FULTON STREET LOOKING EAST TOWARD THE FERRY TERMINAL, CA. 1825 [Opposite]. Schermerhorn Row, looking much as it did when first built, stands at the right. Barrels on the stone-flagged sidewalks are typical of commercial clutter. 19th-century descriptions of the waterfront streets assure us that the scavenging pig is not out of place here. The scoop-bonneted woman gathering her spilled apples may be a street vendor who will sell her fruit from door to door, but the young man who flies his kite from the middle of Fulton Street was probably imagined by the artist. In 1793, when Peter Schermerhorn the Elder bought the land where the twelve buildings comprising the Row now stand, the ground was covered by salt tide twice a day. To make his water lot more useful, Schermerhorn had to build it up by landfill—constructing wooden cribs into which cartmen dumped load after load of soil and refuse. The process of filling and settling took 18 years, and by 1811 construction had begun at the eastern end of the lot. The rest of

the Row followed in 1812, and by the next year Schermerhorn had leased the countinghouses and lofts to merchant firms. Architecturally, the handsome utilitarian Row combines elements of the Georgian and Federal styles. The round-arched doorways seen in the print are trimmed with brownstone blocks at imposts and keystones; the windows have splayed brownstone lintels. The walls are a soft, light-colored brick which could have come from kilns along the Hudson River, but they could have been painted red or cream-color in the fashion of the day.

FULTON STREET AND SCHERMERHORN ROW (NOS. 2–18 FULTON STREET; 91–93 SOUTH STREET; 195 & 197 FRONT STREET), [Above]. Time has wrought changes on Fulton Street since the view of 1825 was drawn. The Row's old countinghouses are still there, but the relationship between the street and the river has altered drastically—the street is now cut off by the East River Drive running overhead. The cobra-headed lamp on the Front Street corner (lower left) stands where the oil lamp stood in 1825.

SCHERMERHORN ROW AND ITS JOHN STREET NEIGHBORS [Opposite]. This aerial view shows Schermerhorn Row at the left side of the center block. Originally roofed with gray slates, the Row now has tar-paper rolls, some of it weathered to silvery brightness. Peter Schermerhorn chose his land well when he built his countinghouses, for hardly had the buildings been roofed and rented than the Brooklyn steam ferry established Fulton Street as its Manhattan terminus. In 1822 the Fulton Market opened on the north side of Fulton Street, attracting crowds each morning to shop for the day's foodstuffs. Thus the Schermerhorn buildings grew in value and while most of the first occupants were merchants, later tenants included grocers, provisioners, eating houses, hotels, liquor shops, taverns, clothiers, bootmakers and barbers.

SWEET'S RESTAURANT, NO. 2 FULTON STREET [Above]. Abraham M. Sweet, who called himself a "victualler," opened his restaurant in Schermerhorn Row, at No. 8 Fulton Street, in 1847. By 1871 the successful eating house had expanded into its present location at No. 2 Fulton Street. Today, with its well deserved reputation as one of New York's best places for seafood, Sweet's is busy every weekday at lunchtime. The "South Street" sign between the windows at the back of the room is a city street marker of a handsome, discontinued type. The fan-shaped, wood-spindled window ornaments are thought to date from a late 19th-century redecoration.

SCHERMERHORN ROW, WEST END [Above]. Peter Schermerhorn's Row was designed as a business block. It had a specialized commercial function in a day when many of the city's merchants still ran stores and businesses from their houses. Shortly after the Revolution, men began to build countinghouses away from home, and when the commercial boom came after the War of 1812, New York was ready with block after block of stores and warehouses much like Schermerhorn Row. The new buildings were a symbol of a great new phase in the city's commercial development. The world's goods passed through them at a faster pace and in larger volume than ever before. Schermerhorn Row is the last block of these early countinghouses remaining in New York. The Row's importance to us is due as much to its place in the city's history as it is to the handsome style in which it was built.

WEST END OF SCHERMERHORN ROW, SEEN FROM THE NORTH ALONG FRONT STREET [Opposite]. The architectural history of any commercial building during 160 active years is one of ceaseless modification as business grows and changes. This has been true of Schermerhorn Row from the early days of its life. Each building was designed to have a wareroom and possibly a countinghouse on its ground floor, with another countinghouse on the second floor that could be reached by an exterior staircase if a barrel-crowded wareroom made access to the interior stairs difficult. By the 1840s the Row's exterior stairs were gone and many of the original arched-door ground-floor facades were replaced by the granite piers of the Greek Revival. The new fronts allowed freer flow of goods and people between the sidewalk and the store, and let light reach the shadowy room within. Most of the ground-floor facades that remain today consist of Victorian cast-iron piers, slimmer still than Greek Revival granite.

SCHERMERHORN ROW, EAST END [Opposite]. The mansard roof over the corner building (No. 2 Fulton Street) replaced the original hipped roof in 1868 when John McKinley prepared to open his steamboat hotel. The Fulton Ferry, which docked a few feet from here, was one of the major entrances to the city, so this corner knew heavy traffic from 1814 until 1924 as the ferry plied its route.

Turn riverward on Fulton Street, then south (right) into South Street.

SOUTH STREET LOOKING SOUTH TOWARD JOHN STREET (BURLING SLIP) [Right]. The three buildings still standing on this block, Nos. 91 through 93 South Street, are Schermerhorn Row's eastern end. No. 92 was part of McKinley's ferry hotel and the mansard roof that covers No. 2 Fulton Street rounds the corner to cover No. 92 South Street as well. Sloppy Louie's seafood restaurant, deservedly popular for shad and other specialties, occupies the first two floors today. Beyond the Schermerhorn Row buildings, a gas station occupies the corner lot on John Street (Burling Slip) where another group of buildings stood from 1811 until 1956. In the vanished corner building was the office of E. K. Collins, founder of the once-famous Collins Line of transatlantic passenger steamships that rivaled England's Cunard Line. The disastrous sinking of Collins' *Arctic* in 1854 nearly ruined the business, then another of its ships simply disappeared. The financial panic of 1857 brought final disaster to Collins, and after that no American passenger line ever challenged the prestige of Cunard.

Walk into the wide expanse of John Street. Burling Slip originally ran down the middle of the street and was flanked on both sides by wharves. In 1835 the slip was filled in, creating a street of unusual width.

JOHN STREET (BURLING SLIP) LOOKING WEST FROM SOUTH STREET, CA. 1865 [Opposite, Top]. When this photograph was taken, a photographer and his equipment were still novelties and people would drop their work to pose. The men of A. A. Low & Brothers, China merchants, stand in windows and doors of the large countinghouse second from the right. (The top-hatted men in the half-opened right-hand door are probably the merchants themselves.) Members of the firm of T. & G. Rowe stand before their linseed oil stores. The firm's ten-bay building had been built in 1835 for commission merchants Mackie, Oakley & Jennison. At that time No. 165, at the center of the block and dating from 1811, was altered to conform with the others. No. 165 was again remodeled in 1840. (Photograph courtesy Museum of the City of New York.)

NOS. 159–171 JOHN STREET (BURLING SLIP) [Opposite, Bottom]. Although the corner building on South Street with the steeply pitched roof has been demolished, this part of the block at the foot of John Street looks much as it did in 1865. The classical attic story of Nos. 159–163 was added in 1917. The building on the right is still recognizable as the countinghouse of A. A. Low & Brothers. The brownstone-fronted building of 1850 is now covered with gray stucco and the cast-iron double storefront, made by Daniel D. Badger, has lost its leafy Corinthian capitals and its metal rolling shutters.

NOS. 159–165 JOHN STREET (BURLING SLIP) [Above]. Architects of the Greek Revival intended their buildings to look like this—a rhythmic march of angular granite piers and lintels giving solid monumentality to the streetscape. The old wooden doors, sash window and cellar bulkhead of No. 165 (right), all visible in the 1865 photograph, probably date from the remodeling of 1840.

10

NOS. 170–176 JOHN STREET (BURLING SLIP) [Opposite]. Greek Revival warehouses with full granite fronts like this one were once plentiful on New York's commercial streets—this is the last one left. In 1840 commission merchant Hickson W. Field built this triple store with a narrow ell (out of view to the left) fronting on high-priced South Street. The Baker, Carver & Morrell ship chandlery has done an excellent job on the restoration of the granite warehouse. They use it today as it was built to be used: fast-moving goods on the ground floor, offices on the second floor and warehousing above.

Turn right onto Front Street.

FRONT STREET, EAST SIDE BETWEEN FULTON STREET AND JOHN STREET (BURLING SLIP) [Above]. A vivid mix of nearly every style of 19th-century waterfront building makes this segment of Front Street visually lively. The two buildings on the left corner (No. 195 Front Street and No. 18 Fulton Street) belong to the 1812 portion of Schermerhorn Row. The pair at the center (Nos. 193 and 191) stand on the site of two small late 18th-century buildings. Those buildings, if they exist today at all, are now submerged in the bricks and mortar of 19th-century alterations. The facades they show today have the Victorian machine-pressed brick and cast-metal trim of the 1870s. The group at the right-hand corner (Nos. 189 and 181 Front Street) is part of the old Mackie, Oakley & Jennison group on John Street.

11

NOS. 191 & 193 FRONT STREET [Above, Left]. The left-hand storefront (No. 193) was made at New York's Atlantic Iron Works on East 12th Street. Its Victorian cast-iron capital is decorated with stylized anthemia. At No. 191 a paneled pilaster has a lacy scrolled cartouche and the remains of a foliate capital.

NO. 18 FULTON STREET (CORNER ON FRONT STREET) [Above, Right]. The graceful thrust of his sword a little like a ship's bowsprit, a swordfish leaps through painted waves on the once-drab bricked-in wall of the retail fish store at the corner of Front and Fulton Streets.

Turn left onto Fulton Street.

NOS. 21, 23 & 25 FULTON STREET [Opposite]. Scaffolding screens the fronts of these buildings as a gentle cleaning removes a century's soot and paint that had begrimed the bricks. Built in 1845–46, the stores are late examples of the Greek Revival style. Like the 1835 buildings on Front and John Streets, these have trabeated (post and lintel) granite ground floors, but here the capitals have a heavy concave profile that is somewhat Egyptian in feeling. The South Street Museum's Book and Chart Store is at No. 25 Fulton Street, on the left-hand corner, and an exhibition gallery has opened at No. 21 (right).

14

BELGIAN-BLOCK PAVING ON FULTON STREET [Opposite]. Grayish-brown, about the size and shape of a loaf of bread, Belgian blocks like these replaced the round, brown cobblestones on city streets during the 1870s and 80s. Though called Belgian blocks, most of these stones came from New England quarries. The pavement's name refers to the tradition that the technique was a Belgian invention. Fulton was one of the first streets to be repaved; its blocks were laid in 1854.

EDMUND MARCH BLUNT'S BOOK AND CHART STORE, CA. 1815 [Above, Left]. Diagonally across Water Street from South Street's Book and Chart Store, on a tiny portion of the site now occupied by the 127 John Street skyscraper, stood Edmund Blunt's famous nautical bookstore "at the sign of the quadrant."

HOLT'S HOTEL, 1833 [Above, Right]. New York in the 19th century was "a paradise of hotels," and the one that started it all was Holt's, built on the site of Blunt's store in 1833. It had marble-faced walls, 225 rooms and a dining room that seated 1000 people. "One of the wonders of the new world," it boasted New York's first steam-powered elevator, which was used to hoist guests' luggage to upper-floor rooms. Later renamed the United States Hotel, the building stood until 1902, when it was replaced by the brick structure that preceded today's gleaming 127 John Street Building.

NO. 127 JOHN STREET [Opposite]. A behemoth of a
building (here seen as a backdrop to Schermerhorn Row),
the structure was built in 1971 by Emery Roth & Sons with
the participation of other artists and designers. The dra-
matic juxtaposition of the skyscraper office building with
the weathered brick warehouses of the Row illustrates the
tremendous growth in scale of New York's trade and architecture since the early 19th century. At the right is the top of
the Woolworth Building (1913).

NO. 127 JOHN STREET [Above]. Its patios and terraces
full of bright-colored chairs and awnings, the 127 John
Street Building is one of a growing group of new office
buildings whose designers have lavished care and imagina-
tion on the buildings' public spaces. This scene in the early
fall, with workers lured onto the plaza to enjoy the sun
during their lunch hour, shows how well the building's design works.

17

LOOKING FROM NO. 127 JOHN STREET TOWARD WATER STREET [Opposite]. Bright canvas awnings are stretched between poles to shade the conversation seats on the Water Street terrace while a pool with fountain bubbles invitingly. The buildings in the background are on Water Street, near the corner of Fulton. The corner building, with scaffolding girding its ground floor (also seen on page 13), is being carefully cleaned.

NO. 127 JOHN STREET [Right]. This whimsical pair of sea people are at home on Fulton Street, just two blocks inland from the Fish Market.

NO. 127 JOHN STREET [Above]. Color is an experience of impressive intensity at the 127 John Street Building. The elevator lobby is entered through a blue-lighted tunnel of corrugated metal; the elevators themselves are painted, carpeted and lighted in red.

NO. 127 JOHN STREET [Above]. The 127 John Street Building is fun to look at, a delight to walk through and a colorful neighbor for a historic district to have. People coming to South Street can detour through its blue tunnel, check watches against the billboard-size digital clock, or climb on the jungle-gym structure that supports the colorful awnings on Fulton Street.

WATER STREET, EAST SIDE, BE-
TWEEN BEEKMAN AND FULTON
STREETS [Opposite]. The three-story
yellow-brick building far left was built
in 1914. It covers the 18th-century wa-
ter-lot holdings of the Livingston fam-
ily. Built for fish market use, it replaced several small old buildings.
Standing next to it, at Nos. 213–215
Water Street, is an Italianate warehouse built for a firm of metal and tin
dealers in 1868 by architect S. D.
Hatch. Ironically, although its ground-
floor front is cast iron, the upper floors
are faced with limestone carved to resemble cast iron—and cast iron had
originally been designed to imitate
carved stone! Chalked lines on its
ground floor represent an effort to re-
construct what the building's missing
storefront detail might have been. The
Greek Revival row at the right, Nos.
207–211 Water Street, was built in
1835 for separate owners. Their builder
may have been David Louderback, a
mason and the owner of No. 211.
Stores like this row, with ground floors
of hewn granite, were introduced to
New York by Ithiel Town in 1829, and
by 1835 they were taking the city's
commercial streets by storm.

NO. 211 WATER STREET [Right].
David Louderback's granite-faced
store, after nearly a century and a half
of use ranging from stove emporium to
meat-packing plant, was the South
Street Seaport Museum's first restoration (1973). The facade was washed
and steamed, and the original ground-
floor window sash was repaired. The
new ground-floor doors and shop window were carefully designed to resemble typical period woodwork. Inside,
an operating printer and stationer's
business works iron hand and treadle
presses to finish jobs its 19th-century
prototypes would have been able to
handle.

211 WATER STREET; CELLAR ENTRANCE [Above].
The granite rainbasin beneath the downspout was heaved and mortared into place as the building went up in 1835. Heavy rains sent water splashing down to the street from its shallow pool and troughs, making mud of the dirt and dust of the days before street cleaning was frequent.

Continue north on Water Street, passing Beekman Street.

VIEW LOOKING NORTH ALONG THE EAST RIVER SHORE [Opposite]. These commercial blocks once derived their value from the docks that extended from South Street into the East River harbor. Tall wind-ships tied at them to unload goods for the city's trade. The docks remain, but the East River Drive cuts them off from the old warehouses. A sturdy stone-faced Gothic Revival pier of the Brooklyn Bridge (1870–83) stands in the river. Further upriver is the sleeker span of the Manhattan Bridge (1909) and, beyond that, is the Williamsburg Bridge (1903). Water Street cuts across the lower left corner of the picture, intersected in the foreground by Beekman Street, next by Peck Slip, and then finally terminated by the highway lanes sweeping into the entrance to the Brooklyn Bridge near City Hall.

VIEW WESTWARD PAST THE ROOF OF NO. 231 WATER STREET [Above]. The use of structural steel and high-speed elevators facilitated an overwhelming change in New York architecture. No. 231 Water Street (seen here from the rear) was built in 1827 and made taller during the third quarter of the 19th century. Beyond it soars Cass Gilbert's 729-foot-tall Woolworth Building. Erected in 1913 in the Gothic Eclectic style, it was the world's tallest building until 1930.

NO. 243 WATER STREET [Above]. This brownstone-quoined surround once opened to a narrow passageway that led between a pair of stores to a courtyard at the center of the block. Records suggest that the stores were built in 1799–1800 for shipchandler Peter Schermerhorn, Schermerhorn Row's developer: No. 243 (left) was his own store and countinghouse. The brick used to face the building's front, though obscured by flaking paint and grime, is unusually firm and regular for the 18th century. It is likely that Schermerhorn imported the prized "best brick" from a Philadelphia kiln.

LOOKING EAST TOWARD WATER STREET FROM THE NORTH SIDE OF PECK SLIP [Above]. Romanesque Revival No. 251 Water Street, built by Carl F. Eisenach in 1888, stands in the foreground, on the southeast corner of Peck Slip. Next to it, at Nos. 247–249 Water Street, is the Greek Revival store built in 1837 for coppersmith Samuel Thompson. No. 245, a pale-painted building of 1836 with a heavy metal cornice added later, was also a coppersmith's store. Uriah Hendricks was its first owner in 1836; his firm specialized in copper boilers for the steam-powered locomotives of the earliest railroads. Beyond the Hendricks store stands Peter Schermerhorn's four-story chandlery. The two-story structure beyond that is the chandlery's twin whose upper stories were taken down in 1941.

NO. 251 WATER STREET [Above]. Green weeds and nameless litter beneath a course of terra-cotta foliage look oddly garden-like as the morning sun lights the face of Romanesque Revival No. 251 Water Street on Peck Slip.

NO. 251 WATER STREET [Opposite]. This rich tan terra-cotta panel, cast with sinuous foliate motifs, decorates an arched doorway in the ground-floor wall of the 1888 building. The specially molded, rounded bricks above the panel form an archivolt defining the doorway's shape.

Cross Peck Slip, one of the principal wharves in the city in 1789, on Water Street.

LOOKING TOWARD THE SOUTH SIDE OF PECK SLIP [Above]. Meyer's Hotel, built by John B. Snook in 1873, stands at the corner of Peck Slip and South Street (far left). The three buildings to its right were built perhaps for use as drygoods warehouses in 1813, four years before the slip was filled in and paved. The store on the far corner of Front Street was built for flour merchants in 1828–29, and the one on the near corner went up in 1827 for grocer Edward G. Faile. Both were made taller in the last decades of the 19th century. The five-story pair at mid-block, apparently built in the 1820s, were rebuilt as stores with tenements on the upper floors in the 1870s. The corner building, No. 251 Water Street, was built for the same purpose in 1888.

NO. 271 WATER STREET [Opposite]. Built in 1875 with a cast-iron ground-floor front and machine-pressed brick facade, No. 271 Water Street still has its full complement of "fire-proof" iron window shutters. Heavy shutters like these, hung in place by strap hinges on iron pintles, were put on warehouse windows as a safety measure. When this building was in active use the shutters would have been swung open at the start of every working day, and pulled and fastened shut at the close. Down at the ground floor an original wooden door, its paneled night shutters firmly nailed into place, fills the right-hand bay.

NO. 273 WATER STREET [Above]. This worn and battered four-story building incorporates the surviving elements of a three-story house built on the waterfront for Captain Joseph Rose. The mariner-merchant bought his land in 1771, and early records suggest two possible construction dates for the house: ca. 1780 or ca. 1797. Before the landfill program of the early 19th century created first Front Street and then South Street, the water came to Rose's backyard where he built a wharf for his brig *Industry*. To the left of the Rose house, at No. 275 stands a metal-fronted warehouse of 1896.

WATER STREET, WEST SIDE, LOOKING NORTH TOWARD THE BROOKLYN BRIDGE [Left]. Water Street has been very quiet in recent years along the block that leads to the Brooklyn Bridge's pylons, but little by little it is coming back to life. No. 270 (in the center with a fire escape), once a rag warehouse for Cyrus Field's famous paper factory, now houses an art gallery and loft apartments.

LOOKING NORTHEAST TOWARD DOVER STREET AND THE BROOKLYN BRIDGE [Opposite]. The span of the Brooklyn Bridge has arched beside Dover Street for nearly a century, but the modern elevated roadbed curving toward the bridge brings the roar of traffic closer than ever before. The construction date of the little wooden building on the corner of Dover and Water Streets is not known for sure, but it was already old when it was remodeled in 1888. The five-story brick building to the right was built in 1881.

LOOKING WEST FROM THE WINDOW OF NO. 279 WATER STREET [Above]. Framed in the window of a restaurant housed in the wooden building at the corner of Dover and Water Streets are the upper stories and tower of the Municipal Building (1914) and the sloping roadway over the pylon of the Brooklyn Bridge. Shuttered windows within the bridge's arches ventilate lofty old warehouses that occupy most of the pylon's spaces.

DOVER STREET, SOUTH SIDE, BETWEEN FRONT AND WATER STREETS [Above]. A rubber-booted man from the fish market strides along Dover Street past a little brick boardinghouse of 1827. Its upper floors are laid in Flemish bond (courses alternating the short ends of the bricks with the long ends) and its ground-floor granite piers are a Greek Revival modernization.

Turn into Front Street, heading south.

You are standing in the block where the "great conflagration" of December 27, 1853, broke out in the "Novelty Bakery" establishment at today's No. 243 Front Street, ruining many of the buildings on this street front and on Water and South Streets. Even more disastrously the fire burned to the water line the celebrated **Great Republic,** *the largest sailing ship in the world. She had been launched just two months before from the East Boston shipyard of Donald McKay, and was bound on her maiden voyage to Liverpool. She had been docked near the foot of Dover Street since late November taking on cargo. While on public exhibition at her berth, the* Great Republic *had netted a considerable income by admitting on board around* **40,000** *spectators who had come to South Street to see her at the rate of twelve and a half cents a person.*

At about 1:00 a.m. on the freezing cold morning of December 27th the bakery fire was discovered. By the time the fire companies arrived, the blaze had spread next door. Defying the firemen's efforts, the flames had soon gone through to Water Street, then across to the east side of Front Street and through the block to South Street. From there it was only a matter of time and wind before the news in the "Fourth Dispatch" to the New York Times *became inevitable: "The fire is still raging with unabated violence. . . . The mammoth clipper,* **The Great Republic,** *is on fire, and will in all probability be totally destroyed!" Still later came the report that heralded her doom ". . . the masts have fallen and the deck is burning."*

Next day, the pyrophile reporter wrote her requiem: "A ship on fire at any time is a grand scene, but the appearance is very remarkable when contrasted with the dark sky of early morning. The falling masts of the **Great Republic** *was a sight than which nothing could be more magnificent."*

The *Great Republic* [above], fully rigged and ready for her maiden voyage, lies at anchor in Boston or New York late in 1853.

FRONT STREET, WEST SIDE, LOOKING SOUTH TO PECK SLIP [Above]. With heavy construction for a Con Edison transformer station underway on its unseen side, narrow Front Street's stone pavements are as muddy and strewn with obstacles as they must have been in the 19th century, when street cleaning was minimal. Stores like those on the right would have had doors thrown open to the sidewalks while a noisy battalion of clerks and cartmen would have jammed the street with crated goods. The building at the far right (half-shown) was built for Thomas Stagg in 1801–02, when Front Street faced the river. The rest of the buildings on the block seem to replace stores burnt in the *Great Republic* fire; several of them housed shipbread bakeries. The towering spire (left) crowns the Cities Service Building (1932) at No. 70 Pine Street. The sleek, boxy building is No. 80 Pine Street.

NO. 250 FRONT STREET [Opposite]. Built anew after the 1853 fire, the building has one of South Street's rare 19th-century shopfronts. Its cast-iron elements were made by the Atlantic Iron Works, whose East 12th Street foundry was near the North River. The beautiful paneled doors would have been made by a city sash-and-door company. Above the shopfront, the facade is faced in smooth, bondless brick. The window lintels are Italianate "eyebrows" in pressed metal. The many-paned sash appears to be a turn-of-the-century alteration.

PECK SLIP, LOOKING WEST PAST FRONT STREET [Above]. The South Street neighborhood, where vision can soar unblocked over the tops of low brick warehouses, offers one of the best views of the downtown skyscrapers. The two tall slabs (center) are the towers of the World Trade Center, built over the span of about a decade by Minoru Yamasaki & Associates with Emery Roth & Sons. To the right are the apartments of Southbridge Towers, a residential complex that has brought people downtown to live after a century of nightly desertion. Just to the right is the Renaissance-inspired tower of the 1915 Transportation Building. At the extreme right, the spire of the Woolworth Building frames the view.

PECK SLIP, LOOKING SOUTH FROM THE
NORTHEAST CORNER OF FRONT STREET
[Opposite]. In this neighborhood of narrow streets,
the wide expanses of the old slips are the sunniest
places. A produce market stood at Peck Slip's inter-
section with Water Street (out of the picture to the
right) in Revolutionary times. The building housing
Meyer's Hotel, built for an undetermined purpose
in 1873, is on the South Street corner. Throughout
most of the 18th century, Peck Slip was one of New
York's most active areas; here the ferry from Brooklyn had its dock, and here the Long Island farm
boats would land, their decks loaded with garden
goods for market. Toward the end of the century,
however, trade changed, and the broad-beamed
little boats that could use the slips were outmoded
by sleeker, deep-draft vessels for which piers had
to be run out into the river itself. Most of the city's
old slips had been filled in and forgotten by 1800,

but Peck Slip, probably because small farm boats
still used it, stayed open until 1817. Thus the two
buildings to the right of Meyer's Hotel, put up in
1813 for John and William Mott, were standing before Peck Slip became a paved street.

Walk along Front Street past Peck Slip.

LOOKING TOWARD THE NORTH SIDE OF
PECK SLIP AND SOUTH STREET, 1857
[Above]. The wooden awning poles (lower right)
stand in front of the Mott warehouses on Peck Slip;
the barrels littering the street await a clerk to roll
them to storage inside. The four-story building at
the corner of South Street (No. 151) stands alone
today. Its neighbors (shown here in an illustration
from *Valentine's Manual,* 1857) were demolished in
1962.

NO. 235 FRONT STREET, SOUTHEAST CORNER OF PECK SLIP [Opposite]. Flour merchants Wood & Birdsall had this corner building put up in 1828–29 to replace an earlier store they had occupied on the same site. Its walls are laid up with handmade brick in Flemish bond, and this graceful Federal-style doorway remains on Peck Slip. The arch is turned in gauged brick, with a double keystone and impost blocks of brownstone, but someone has closed it recently with a cement-block wall. The scrolled wrought-iron balcony casting a lacy shadow on the wall was put up as part of a fire escape late in the 19th century.

FRONT STREET, EAST SIDE, LOOKING NORTH TO-WARD PECK SLIP [Above]. The steel framework beyond Peck Slip marks construction of Con Edison's new trans-former station, which will be brick-faced and slope-roofed to complement the neighborhood's old brick warehouses. The design reflects a close cooperation between Con Edison's management and the South Street Seaport Museum. On the near corner of Front Street stands the 1828 store of Wood & Birdsall; next to it is No. 233 Front Street, a four-story, dormer-windowed building erected in 1828–29 and first occupied by grocers Hopkins & Hawley. Ten years after their first building was finished, Hopkins & Hawley built a new store next door at No. 231 (far right)—one of the handsomest Greek Revival stores left in New York. Its staunch granite piers are heavier than those of most store-fronts, but like other granite piers, they were probably cut and finished at a New England quarry, then shipped down the coast on a specially rigged stone sloop.

NO. 228 FRONT STREET [Left]. Oyster merchant George M. Still's painted sign at No. 228 is one of the neighborhood's best. Serifed and shadowed letters make good use of the panel on the cast-iron pier. Although the building may incorporate a double store dating from 1830, the cast-iron piers of the storefront may have been added in the mid 1860s, when a bakery was housed here. Mr. Still's painted truck, decorated with skill and vigor equal to this lettering, often stands in front of the store.

NOS. 220–224 FRONT STREET [Opposite]. These five-story stores stand on the site of stores built around 1799 for Ebenezer Stevens (timber merchant and veteran of the Revolution) and Peter Schermerhorn (ship-chandler and builder of Schermerhorn Row). Evidence suggests that elements of the early buildings remain within the structures today, although the group's appearance is Victorian. No. 220 (left) was given its top three floors and its iron shopfront in 1855. Remarkably, the shopfront remains, its peeling wooden night shutters as they were more than a century ago and the iron window paneless, but otherwise complete. Visible above the empty lot at the left is the spire of the Woolworth Building.

NO. 220 FRONT STREET [Opposite]. An unlikely but far from uncommon set of circumstances has created tiny garden pockets throughout the South Street neighborhood, and summer observers have come to expect alfalfa fringes on certain crumbling cornices, or ferns like this one flourishing in brownstone at No. 220 Front Street. The window frame below the fern is fireproof cast iron, as is the shutter firmly closed inside it.

NO. 220 FRONT STREET [Above]. Against the wall of a new neighbor the "ghost" of No. 218 Front Street, built during the 1820s, is clearly marked. The heavily mortared bricks of its side wall remain today as part of the neighbor's wall. At least this much of the demolished building will stand as long as No. 220 does.

FRONT STREET, NEAR NO. 214 [Above]. Carts just like this one—sometimes drawn by men, sometimes by horses—appear in prints two hundred years old. A century ago visitors to the city wrote that the streets were so full of such carts that a pedestrian trying to cross took his life in his hands.

FRONT STREET, LOOKING TOWARD THE NORTH-
EAST CORNER OF BEEKMAN STREET [Above]. With
its cockle-shell cornice and starfish tie-rod ends, the building on the northeast corner of Front and Beekman Streets
(left) is jubilantly symbolic of the Fulton Fish Market,
which was enjoying a high moment in its history when this
structure was built for one of Peter Schermerhorn's descen-
dants in 1885. George B. Post designed it, as well as the two
buildings adjoining it on Beekman Street (1884). At the far
right, beyond the elevated East River Drive, is the Fulton
Fish Market (1907), known today as "the old shed." It was
on that site that the first wooden shed was built in 1835 for
the fish sellers of the Fulton Market. At that site they have
worked continuously ever since.

NO. 211 FRONT STREET (142 BEEKMAN STREET) [Left]. Fanciful scallops, starfish and vigorously modeled fish, all symbolic of the Fulton Fish Market, ornament the walls and windows of the building. The machine-made brick used here, dating from the 1880s, is smooth and perfect; its mason laid it up elegantly with narrow "buttered" joints, the sleekest kind he could work.

BEEKMAN STREET, NORTH SIDE, BETWEEN FRONT AND SOUTH STREETS [Opposite]. Old painted signs, flaked from weathering and growing fainter every day, abound in this market district where businesses have been operating so long that new signs seem like an extravagance. Another typical sight is the truck pulled up next to a cooper's stall, collecting repaired crates for the next day's fish packing. At the corner of the block, next to the two buildings by Post, is a store that may date in part from 1823. Its wooden-post awnings are of a type that fell into disuse when trucks became common.

BEEKMAN STREET, LOOKING WEST PAST FRONT STREET [Opposite]. Seagulls stand on the cornice of No. 212 Front Street (1824). Its gambrel-roofed neighbor dates from 1882. Above the rough-walled warehouses rise the top of the Municipal Building's tower—a milk-white "temple of love" topped by the gilded figure of Civic Fame. McKim, Mead & White were the building's architects. Through their ingenious design the skyscraper, completed in 1914, spans busy Chambers Street like a triumphal arch.

BEEKMAN STREET, LOOKING WEST PAST FRONT STREET [Right]. Beekman Street was opened to the waterfront in 1824 to provide access to a busy place known as the Crane Wharf. The building at the left, No. 212 Front Street, was built the same year the street went through for grocers Joseph and Elias Drake. Its arch-pierced ground floor is characteristic of New York stores of the 1820s. The rusticated white stucco on the ground floor is modern, but the original brownstone arches survive beneath it on the Beekman Street side.

Continuing south on Front Street, you pass on the east the rear of the Fulton Market block.

FULTON STREET AND MARKET, FROM *MEGAREY'S STREET VIEWS,* 1828–33 [Above]. Fulton Market was opened in this classical structure (right) in 1822, and it immediately became one of New York's busiest food markets. Here Fulton Street is full of tradesmen and wheeled carts.

Along the sidewalk stride the silk-hatted merchants and shoppers on their way to market. In this view Fulton Street is still cobbled, and Schermerhorn Row still has its original round-arched entrances, exterior stairways and paneled shutters. (Courtesy Museum of the City of New York.)

FULTON STREET, LOOKING NORTH TO FRONT STREET [Above]. Waiting for midday business, a hot-dog vendor rests in the shadow of Schermerhorn Row. Today's Fulton Market (the third structure of that name, built in 1953) stretches north along Front Street, the scaly arrow-shaped fish pointing the way to the entrance. The blank sidewall behind the hot-dog man is part of No. 203 Front Street, its fading sign advertising the business of Winant & Co., oyster sellers and the building's last fish merchant occupants. Above the Beekman Street buildings, the Brooklyn Bridge tower supports the graceful webbing that suspends the heavy roadbed.

FRONT STREET, WEST SIDE, LOOKING NORTH FROM FULTON STREET TOWARD DOVER STREET [Above]. These Front Street buildings—all altered more than once—went up around the beginning of the 19th century, after the street had been paved and opened to Peck Slip in 1797. With the exception of the 1914 warehouse at the far end of the block, all were the first permanent buildings on their sites (several replaced older wooden buildings). No.

203 and No. 204 (left), built separately, were remodeled together in 1882 to become a waterfront hotel. No. 205, an earlier building, received its Greek Revival granite-pillared ground floor during the 1830s or 40s. No. 206 has a late 19th-century front, built after a major fire; at No. 207 a tall peaked roof survives from the early 19th century with a wooden hoisting wheel fixed just under its ridge.

NO. 203 FRONT STREET [Above]. Clouds are reflected in the new glass transoms over Victorian-style doors reproduced from an 1882 architect's drawing of this building. Theobald Engelhardt remodeled it and its neighbor (No. 204) as a waterfront hotel, and the ground floor front was restored to his original specifications in 1974. Careful cleaning of the granite piers revealed traces of a long-ago flour merchant's black-and-gold painted signs. Bollards, normally used to moor ships to docks, here guard the building's front against damage by trucks backing up for loading. The Belgian-block paving on the sidewalk dates from the building's fish market days when the bays across the front were used for loading trucks.

LOOKING NORTHEAST PAST THE BROOKLYN BRIDGE FROM THE ROOF OF NO. 203 FRONT STREET [Opposite]. The rooftops of the seaport buildings are an aspect of the neighborhood that visitors seldom see. Here the Victorian roofs of No. 203–204 Front Street (foreground) slant gently down to the parapet formed by the top of the bold, projecting cornice. Across the stepped fire wall is the steeper slope of Greek Revival No. 205, and across from that is the steep pitch of the early 19th-century peak of No. 207. The building facades in the middle ground face Beekman Street. The long, low structure to the right, on the other side of the highway, is the Fulton Fish Market's "new" building, dating from the mid-1930s. Arching above them all are two of the downtown bridges—the Brooklyn Bridge nearer, then the Manhattan Bridge.

NO. 207 FRONT STREET [Right]. Forgotten for nearly a hundred years in the loft of No. 207 Front Street, this enormous wheel (about ten feet in diameter) once operated the hoisting mechanism essential to upper-floor storage in these waterfront warehouses. Other peak-roofed buildings here have managed to retain these ancient mechanical devices.

MANHATTAN BRIDGE PYLON, PIKE SLIP AND WATER STREET [Opposite]. The Manhattan Bridge, completed in 1909, reflects the perfect union between style and utility so often found in the structures of the early 20th century. While engineer Gustav Lindenthal worked out the dynamics of the powerful suspension system, the firm of Carrère & Hastings, famous for its Beaux Arts architecture, gave the bridge its Renaissance design. The chain-fenced lot in front of the plot is used by the city for storage. The disjointed scraps of metal lying among the weeds and flowers are the components of a cast-iron facade awaiting restoration.

Walk down Fulton Street to South Street, turn left and go

north. *The Fulton Fish Market's "old shed" (1907), on the right, offers one of the city's most breathtaking river views from its east windows. On the left is the third Fulton Market to stand on the site. The E-shaped market of 1822 was open on the South Street side, its courtyard filled with the stalls of the hucksters and "country people." The 1882 market, more compactly built, had a grand High Victorian South Street facade of dark brick and terra cotta. The present building offers only garage-like doors.*

SOUTH STREET AT MAIDEN LANE, FROM *MEGAREY'S STREET VIEWS*, 1834 [Above]. This early view suggests the bustle of men and goods in South Street during a working day.

SOUTH STREET, WEST SIDE, FROM NEAR BEEK-
MAN STREET NORTH TO PECK SLIP [Above]. This
block is the last complete row of South Street's once-re-
nowned countinghouses. Weatherworn and a little dingy
now with their rusty metal awnings, a century and a half
ago they were glorious. Banners fluttered from their upper
stories, ground-floor warerooms were in constant activity,
merchants barked orders at their clerks from platforms at
the rear of second-floor counting rooms. No. 107 South

Street (far left) was originally occupied in 1819 by ship-
chandler Robert T. Hicks. The six-building row (next, to
the right) was built at the same time for Peter Schermerhorn
and Ebenezer Stevens. Beyond that row, the five-story double building at Nos. 114–115 was built in 1840 for the firm of
Slate, Gardiner & Howell. The pedimented corner building
is Meyer's Hotel. Peck Slip is beyond, and across it the steel
framing for Con Edison's Seaport substation is nearly
complete.

64

MEYER'S HOTEL (NOS. 116–119 SOUTH STREET AND NOS. 42–44 PECK SLIP) [Above]. In the days of dazzling waterfront saloons, this hotel and bar was kept by liquor dealer Henry F. Meyer. It was built in 1873 by architect John B. Snook, whose working drawings for it have been preserved. Although it may have been a hotel from the first, Snook's drawings and notes do not specify the building's use, and not until the early 20th century does a specific reference to it as a hotel occur. The sidewalk awning with its wooden posts is an old one, and the late 19th-century bar within is resplendent with carved dark wood and cut and mirrored glass. The little buildings on the right were erected as warehouses in 1813. The skyscraper rising above them is the Cities Service Building at No. 70 Pine Street (1932; Clinton & Russell, architects).

SOUTH STREET, LOOKING SOUTH FROM PECK SLIP TO BEEKMAN STREET, ca. 1855 [Above]. The Fulton Market and Schermerhorn Row appear along South Street in the background. At the far right is Nos. 114–115 South Street, the house of Slate, Gardiner & Howell, commission merchants.

SOUTH STREET, LOOKING SOUTH FROM PECK SLIP TO BEEKMAN STREET [Above]. Fire escapes have replaced the blockmaker's banners, and fish sellers have usurped the place of the commission merchants in the ground-floor stores, but otherwise the buildings on this block of South Street have changed very little since the woodcut of 1855 was engraved. Countinghouse windows, from which merchants surveyed the bustle on the dock, now look out on the elevated East River Drive. The street itself, once filled with the clamor of stages and sailors, is now almost deserted as traffic speeds by on the Drive.

SOUTH STREET, LOOKING SOUTHWEST TOWARD BEEKMAN STREET AND THE FINANCIAL DISTRICT [Above]. Twentieth-century office buildings tower over their 19th-century counterparts. No. 88 Pine Street, its upper corner visible beneath the diagonal of the East River Drive, was built in 1973 by I. M. Pei & Partners. The tall dark building to the right is 80 Pine Street. Next to it, its tower the highest point in the skyline, is the 1932 Cities Service Building at No. 70 Pine Street. Further on, seen only by the top of its steep, four-sided tower, stands the Bank of Manhattan Company Building (now the Manufacturers Hanover Trust Company) built by Craig Severance with Yasuo Matsui in 1929 at No. 40 Wall Street.

NO. 151 SOUTH STREET (NO. 45 PECK SLIP) [Opposite]. Merchant Jasper Ward advertised "a large and convenient Counting-Room to let" when this building was finished in the spring of 1807. It had wharves on two sides then, for Peck Slip (a street now, extending left into the foreground) had not yet been filled in, and the South Street side faced water, too. No. 45 Peck Slip was spared when its South Street neighbors were demolished in 1973 for Con Edison's new station. That its walls, formerly bolstered by buildings on both sides, stood unsupported for two years is a tribute to the wreckers' care and the skill of the original builders.

Turn, walking south on South Street.

Begin the walk back toward Schermerhorn Row, and look toward the water as you walk along the shoreline of New York. "There, now, is your insular city of the Manhattoes," wrote Herman Melville, beginning Moby Dick, *"belted round by wharves as Indian isles by coral reefs—commerce surrounds it with her surf. . . . What do you see? Posted like silent sentinels all around the town, stand thousands upon thousands of mortal men fixed in ocean reveries."*

Today the insular city is belted round not only by her wharves, but by the system of highways which girds the lower quarters of the city between the old marginal streets and the river. The East River Drive has been part of the landscape at South Street for about 30 years, and unless vehicular traffic in lower Manhattan is curtailed, is likely to remain part of the scene. Through the fretwork of its marching stilts, the water view is framed for us.

Walk down Fulton Street, then under the roadway and through the gate to South Street's Piers 15 & 16.

As you come out onto the pier, you'll see the ships ranged along the docks: the ships represent the various phases of the maritime history of this port city.

PIER 16, SEEN FROM ACROSS THE EAST RIVER DRIVE [Opposite]. Although the intrusive elevated highway now stands between the land and the piers, ships still lie here at the open docks. At South Street's Pier 16 there is the clipper-bowed fishing schooner *Lettie G. Howard* (left side, front). One of the last of her kind, she was built in Essex, Massachusetts, in 1893. The big vessel at the center of the left side, with two covered gangplanks leading aboard her, is the former hospital ship now renamed *Robert Fulton*. Behind the barge is the 1908 lightship *Ambrose,* and nestled away from the pier on *Ambrose's* far side is the small 1899 tug *Mathilda.* Along the right side of the pier is the iron-hulled square-rigger *Wavertree,* built in England in 1885.

PIER 16, LOOKING NORTHWEST TO THE FISH MARKET [Above]. The broad planked decks of South Street's piers were extended and rebuilt just after the turn of the century. For many years they were covered with barnlike cargo sheds which have been removed, leaving the piers open to weather as their predecessors were in the 19th century. The covered gangplank goes aboard the *Robert Fulton.* Looking inland, Schermerhorn Row's South Street corner is visible far left, behind the drive. Farther in the distance are the balconied apartments of Southbridge Towers. Between two of the buildings in the complex the cylindrical tower of the Municipal Building is visible. The white structure at the right, with long black vertical rows of windows, is the new New York Telephone building.

LOOKING INLAND FROM PIER 17 [Above]. A disused gangplank frames a view of the old Fulton Fish Market's river side. In the days when fish came to market on schooners like South Street's *Lettie G. Howard,* this pier was a busy place. Since much of today's catch is trucked down from New England at night and delivered to the market's street front, few people find their way around to look at the back. Those who do are able to see, above each bay, the old white-on-blue enameled signs that belonged to this market's first tenants—the firms which occupied these stalls on opening day in February, 1907.

AMBROSE [Opposite]. In her working years, *Ambrose* marked the Ambrose Channel into New York Harbor, an entrance made unpredictable and difficult by shifting sandbars. She served as Coast Guard's first lightship on the Channel from 1908 until 1936, when she took a new position on the Scotland station off Sandy Hook. *Ambrose* came to South Street in 1968, four years after her replacement by a more efficient, but less beautiful, Coast Guard buoy, and was the Museum's first vessel. Beyond the *Ambrose's* masts, the Brooklyn and Manhattan Bridges span the river. On the far shore are Brooklyn's cargo sheds and giant warehouses.

LOOKING UPRIVER FROM *AMBROSE'S* DECK [Opposite]. Tugboat *Mathilda* nestles close by as a couple enjoy the view from *Ambrose*. A big freighter, weighted almost to the waterline, slides downriver with cargo booms bristling above her decks.

LOOKING EAST TOWARD PIER 16 [Above]. There are men living today who tell of bowsprits arching toward warehouse windows on South Street as *Wavertree's* does today. Seventy years ago, however, the river's edge was closer to the street than it is now. The "apron" connecting the piers which these families are walking on was made much wider around 1905.

LOOKING NORTHWEST TOWARD *WAVERTREE* FROM PIER 15 [Above]. The iron-hulled square-rigger *Wavertree* was built for a shipping firm in England in 1885, in the waning days of the age of sail. She worked for a quarter of a century in the nitrate trade, her voyages often taking her to the dusty guano ports on the western coast of South America. Overworked and undermaintained, *Wavertree* was wrecked in a storm off Cape Horn in 1910. Towed to a quiet backwater near Punta Arenas, she was used as a floating warehouse for more than 50 years. In 1970, after three years of work and planning, *Wavertree* was brought to

New York to begin a new life as a museum ship at South Street. The tall building past *Wavertree's* bowsprit is No. 127 John Street.

LOOKING NORTHEAST FROM *WAVERTREE'S* DECK [Opposite]. *Wavertree's* lofty decks are a workmanlike jumble of line, tools and wood as her restoration makes steady progress. Beyond her decks, left, is the former hospital barge renamed *Robert Fulton,* and to the right is the light-ship *Ambrose.* The buildings across the river are in Brooklyn's warehouse district.

PIONEER [Above]. With her black-painted iron hull, Museum schooner *Pioneer* is easy to identify when she is seen under sail. A small coasting schooner built in 1885 to carry iron and steel from a rolling mill to a shipyard on the Delaware River, she was restored and rebuilt in the late 1960s, and was given to the South Street Seaport Museum in 1970. Here she waits at her pier, sails securely fastened between lowered gaff and boom. Dark tufts on her stays are "baggy wrinkles" made of old rope ends wound onto the wires to prevent chafing damage to the sails.

LOOKING EAST TOWARD BROOKLYN FROM *PI-OONEER'S* BOWSPRIT [Above]. Crewmen find firm foot-ing on *Pioneer's* bowsprit shrouds as they work on furling her staysail. The men face cargo sheds on Brooklyn's wharves and their backs are turned to a small visiting vessel which can move under power of both steam and sail. The little hybrid is one of many ships that visit South Street: some of them are square-rigged training ships or other his-toric craft.

LOOKING SOUTH TOWARD THE SKYSCRAPERS OF LOWER MANHATTAN [Opposite]. The tall building far left, No. 55 Water Street, straddles the place where Coenties Slip used to be. The mammoth structure, built in 1973 by Emery Roth & Sons, houses the downtown branch of the Whitney Museum along with businesses. The next building to the right is No. 11 Wall Street. The white, stepped building, No. 120 Wall Street, is a clear reflection of the 1916 zoning laws that required tall buildings to set back their upper floors to allow light to reach the streets below. The tip of the tower seen to the right belongs to No. 20 Exchange Place, built by Cross & Cross in 1931. The architects' design called for an ornate structure to crown the tower, but the stock market crash of 1929 put an end to that extravagant plan.

LOOKING SOUTH ALONG THE WATERFRONT FROM PIER 17 [Above]. Old vessels flank the fringes of the city for a few blocks at South Street. Closest is the foredeck of the water lighter *Aqua*, which originally carried cargo to the docks from deep-draft vessels anchored in the stream, and later carried fresh water to similarly unwieldy vessels. Beyond *Aqua* is the clipper-bowed Gloucesterman *Lettie G. Howard*. The bowsprit striking a smart angle belongs to *Wavertree*. The ships face the elevated East River Drive and the sheer walls of the downtown towers.

BARBA NEGRA [Opposite]. Square-rigged sails on a barkentine's foremast spread to the summer sun during *Barba Negra's* visit to South Street in 1975. This three-masted Canadian vessel is built to resemble a historic ship type.

PIER 15 [Above]. The timeless work of ships clutters South Street's planked piers today as it did in the past. Here crewmen of a visiting square-rigged vessel, in clothing little different than that worn by seamen in the 19th century, splice rope and mend sail.

TITANIC MEMORIAL TOWER, PIER 16 [Opposite]. It may look like a diving bell from a Jules Verne story, but it is really a timepiece. Placed in its original location atop the old Seaman's Church Institute after the sinking of the *Titanic,* the landmark tower memorialized those who died in the wreck. A beacon light shone from its windowed sides, and every day at noon a ball would descend along a pole (not attached now) atop the tower. The *Titanic* tower came to the South Street Seaport Museum after its building was demolished in 1968. Since this photograph was taken it has been moved to its permanent site in the park at Fulton and Water Streets.

BOLLARD, PIER 15 [Right]. Sturdy bollards like this one, tightly bolted to the heavy timbers framing East River piers, once held ropes securing sailing ships to their berths in port. This one, with its traditional styling, is probably about 70 years old.

PIER 15 LOOKING NORTHEAST TOWARD BROOK-
LYN [Above]. On a sunny Saturday at South Street,
yachtsmen gather for a day's sailing in the harbor. Beyond
their small sloops *Pioneer* (1885) is seen at the next pier. The
partly raised sail seen beyond her rigging belongs to the
visiting *Barba Negra.* Brooklyn's Watchtower warehouse
stands on the opposite shore (upper right).

MARKET CAT, PIER 17 [Above]. The streets of the fish market shelter some of the world's oddest cats. Not all are as world-weary as this squashed-eared tom, but all have a taste for the fresh fish waste that is so plentiful around the fish market.

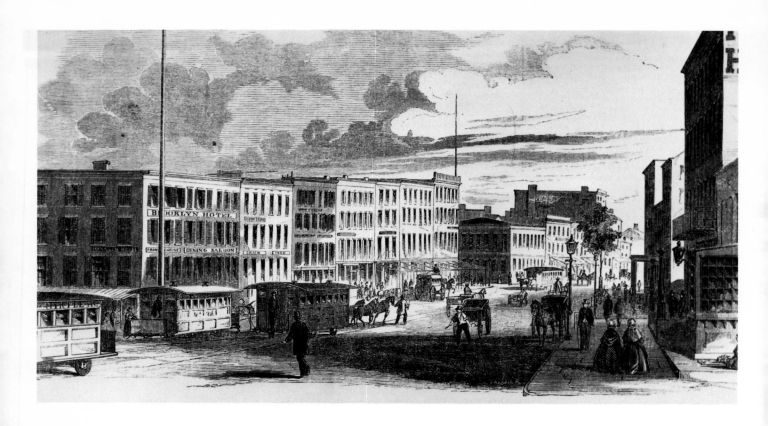

Brooklyn Bridge and Brooklyn.

To understand how Brooklyn grew as a city, you must look at its Fulton Street. The ferry from Fulton Street, Manhattan, landed at its foot, and because of its importance as a thoroughfare a busy commercial center of grocers, coal dealers, cracker bakers and storekeepers began to develop. Fulton Street's old buildings (the earliest surviving ones dating from 1836) are almost identical with their contemporaries at South Street. Their uses, too, were similar. The Victorian trim that bedizens the corner hotel reflects the same flush of prosperity of the 1860s that fitted out the Fulton Ferry Hotel in Schermerhorn Row on the Manhattan side. In 1883 the Brooklyn Bridge opened, and though the ferry ran for another 40 years, Fulton Street was the road to New York City no longer. It was the suddenness and completeness of its commercial demise that left Fulton Street and its historic buildings intact.

LOOKING EAST ALONG FULTON STREET, BROOKLYN, 1857 [Above]. Brooklyn's Fulton Street was just reaching its prime when this view was drawn. Shoppers and merchants make its sidewalks lively while horsecars, coaches and cartmen clatter over the cobbled street.

LOOKING NORTH ON THE EAST RIVER [Opposite]. Beyond the bow of a wooden boat, the graceful sweeps of three great suspension bridges connect Manhattan to Brooklyn. The Brooklyn Bridge, in the foreground, is the oldest of them. Completed in 1883, it was the first alternative to the old ferry service across the East River. Farther up the river is the Manhattan Bridge, opened in 1909; in the distance the Williamsburg Bridge (1903) is visible.

LOOKING SOUTH INTO LOWER MANHATTAN FROM THE BROOKLYN BRIDGE WALKWAY [Left]. High above the river, on the Brooklyn Bridge's pedestrian crossing, walkers have a fine view of the buildings of downtown Manhattan. The rough little steep-roofed warehouses of the South Street area are striking from here, set off as they are by the sheer-walled elegance of the newest buildings.

LOOKING EAST TOWARD BROOKLYN FROM PIER 16 [Above]. A telephoto lens brings Brooklyn's Fulton Street closer to the piers of South Street, and the old stores that line the street are visible against the giant warehouses that form their background. The Fulton Ferry ran from the Brooklyn shore to the photographer's viewing point between 1814 and 1924.

PACE UNIVERSITY, SEEN FROM THE BROOKLYN BRIDGE [Opposite]. Looking back inland from near the Manhattan end of the Brooklyn Bridge, the pedestrian has a fine view of Pace University's handsome new building. Beyond it rise the twin towers of the World Trade Center, designed by a consortium of architects including Minoru Yamasaki and Emery Roth & Sons. To the right is Cass Gilbert's Woolworth Building (1913).

THE BROOKLYN BRIDGE, LOOKING TOWARD MANHATTAN FROM BROOKLYN'S EMPIRE STORES [Above]. The Brooklyn Bridge was conceived and designed in the Gothic Revival style by John Augustus Roebling. In 1869 he was fatally injured while making preliminary observations on the bridge's site. Construction was completed by his son, Washington Roebling, whose health was wrecked by the caisson disease he suffered while working on the foundations of the piers. Since its opening in 1883, the bridge has stood as a monument to the engineering genius of the two men.

FIREBOAT HOUSE AT THE FOOT OF FULTON STREET, BROOKLYN [Opposite]. At the end of Fulton Street the towered wooden fireboat house, built in 1924 and now used as a gallery for historical exhibits, stands at the old Fulton Ferry slip. Just above its roof, to the right of the tower (originally used to hang hoses for drying), is the top of the Brooklyn City Railroad building. The Eagle Warehouse stands to the left. The pile-driving barge in the foreground has made a bulkhead creating new land for Fulton Ferry Park.

LOOKING TOWARD FULTON STREET, BROOKLYN, FROM THE FIREBOAT PIER [Above]. The Fulton Ferry docked in the slip in the right foreground. Across Fulton Street the Eagle Warehouse can be recognized by its corbeled brick cornice. Beyond the tower of the fireboat pier rises the higher turret of the Watchtower warehouse.

FULTON STREET, BROOKLYN [Opposite]. The building on the corner of Water Street has always been a hotel. Built in 1835 and later called the Franklin House, it replaced an earlier inn kept by Gerardus Langdon, who came from South Street across the river. Into the building to the right Langdon moved in 1836 to run a coal and tea store. Inhabitants of this neighborhood live with the constant hum of tires on the bridge's metal roadway.

NORTHEAST SIDE OF FULTON STREET, BROOKLYN [Above]. With the exception of the cast-iron building far right, all of these structures were built between 1835 and 1837. The spacious street retains its old Belgian-block paving stones under a layer of asphalt.

NO. 8 FULTON STREET, BROOKLYN [Opposite]. Morning-glory garlands deck the Furman Street front of the Brooklyn City Railroad Company Building (1860–61),

whose main facade is around the corner on Fulton Street. Tall and elegant, this fine Victorian office building graced the "aristocratic" southwest side of the street whose occupants felt entitled to look condescendingly at the grocers and flour merchants on the "democratic" side. One of the first of many planned restorations for Fulton Street's buildings, No. 8 has been carefully renovated for use as loft apartments.

SOUTHWEST SIDE OF FULTON STREET, BROOKLYN [Above]. These Greek Revival stores, built between 1836 and 1839, housed an intriguing variety of businesses. Fruiterer, saddler, grocers, tea merchant, oyster house—all were here in 1840. The faintest remnants of old painted signs, visible today, tell of a paper dealer who worked from Nos. 13 and 15. The old wooden-poled awnings date from the second half of the 19th century.

NO. 13 FULTON STREET, BROOKLYN [Opposite]. Although these doors are old, they represent a 19th-century modification to this 1836 building. Such doors were made at sash-and-door companies, their parts cut by machine, then assembled by hand. The doorknob is brown-glazed ceramic.

FULTON STREET, BROOKLYN, LOOKING ACROSS THE EAST RIVER TO MANHATTAN [Opposite]. In the days when horse-drawn wagons carried goods to and from warehouses, awnings like this one stretched across the sidewalk to stanchions (supporting posts) near the curb. When the 20th century came, with its onslaught of trucks, the form of the awnings changed. Most seen on commercial streets today are carried on cables fastened to the upper walls of warehouses.

EAGLE WAREHOUSE, FULTON STREET, BROOKLYN [Above]. The Eagle Warehouse is a great Romanesque Revival pile built of dark red brick in 1870 on the site where the *Brooklyn Daily Eagle* was printed through most of the 19th century. Architect Frank Freeman planned this massive arch for the main entrance. It combines a truck roadway and a pedestrian walk behind its fleur-de-lis-spiked bronze gates. Separating road and walkway is a griffin-headed lamppost.

103

EAGLE WAREHOUSE, FULTON STREET, BROOKLYN [Left]. This powerful swooping eagle, cast in zinc, is hidden to all but the sharp-eyed on the Eagle Warehouse's dark brick wall. Much older than the building, the grayed and weathered bird was made for the *Brooklyn Daily Eagle* office which stood on the site.

LONG ISLAND SAFE DEPOSIT COMPANY BUILDING, FULTON STREET, BROOKLYN [Opposite]. Built in 1868–69 by the fashionable architect William Mundell, this cast-iron building was the grandest structure on Fulton Street. Its forms are taken from the Venetian stone palaces of the Renaissance, and though the splendors of its facade are enough to please most building-watchers, it was the structure's vaults that made it unusual. The vaults, into which depositors' valuables were double-locked, were called "separate buildings within a building," with granite foundations and iron walls of their own. You could see them as you walked by on Fulton Street, for they were "kept in full view of everybody in the . . . full blaze of gas-light." The vaults are gone now, and in their place one sees through the grilled windows the colorful wares of a fruit merchant. The three-story brick building (right), built in 1834, housed the Long Island Bank, Brooklyn's first.

EMPIRE STORES, WATER STREET, BROOKLYN
[Above]. The arch-pierced Empire Stores were built as
warehouses for James Nesmith. The first section was
erected in 1869–70; the last was finished in 1880. The Stores
stand along Water Street north of New Dock Street. Sec-
tions of Water Street's old sidewalk, paved with bluestone
slabs, survive in front of the Stores.

EMPIRE STORES, WATER STREET, BROOKLYN
[Opposite]. Pennyroyal, wild aster, goldenrod and grass
grow on the forgotten wharf behind the Empire Stores. The
plants have seeded and thrived here for so many years that
they have made a meadow of a city shore. The projections
above several loading bays held block-and-tackle for hoisting barrels and crates to upper-floor storage. The massive
pylon of the Brooklyn Bridge complements the Romanesque
weightiness of the Stores.

EMPIRE STORES, WATER STREET, BROOKLYN. Broad, round-headed arches turned in brick and secured by strap-hinged iron shutters give the Empire Stores their look of solid monumentality. Star-shaped tie-rod ends and a corbeled brick cornice are the building's only trim. The ropes knotted to rings on the shutters' inner sides were used by workmen inside the loft to swing the shutters closed.

LEARNING RESOURCES CENTER

MONTGOMERY COUNTY COMMUNITY COLLEGE

Cognitio Ad Futurum

1964

BLUE BELL, PENNSYLVANIA